Starwalker

Starwalker

Book, music, and lyrics
by Corey Payette

Starwalker
first published 2025 by Scirocco Drama
An imprint of J. Gordon Shillingford Publishing Inc.
© 2025 Corey Payette

Scirocco Drama Editor: Glenda MacFarlane
Cover design by Doowah Design
Cover photo by Matt Barnes, featuriung Dillan Chiblow. Photoshoot art direction by Andrea Tétrault.
Author photo by Luke Fontana
Production photos by David Cooper Photography

Printed and bound in Canada on 100% post-consumer recycled paper.

Production inquiries to:
https://www.coreypayette.com

Library and Archives Canada Cataloguing in Publication

Title: Starwalker / Corey Payette.
Names: Payette, Corey, 1987- author.
Identifiers: Canadiana 20250183676 | ISBN 9781990738685 (softcover)
Subjects: LCGFT: Drama.
Classification: LCC PS8631.A928 S73 2025 | DDC C812/.6—dc23

J.Gordon Shillingford Publishing respectfully acknowledges that we are located in Winnipeg, which is on Treaty 1 territory, the traditional lands of the Anishinaabe, Cree, Oji-Cree, Dene, and Dakota Peoples, and the homeland of the Métis Nation.

We acknowledge the financial support of the Canada Council for the Arts, the Government of Canada, the Manitoba Arts Council, and the Manitoba Government for our publishing program.

J. Gordon Shillingford Publishing
P.O. Box 86, RPO Corydon Avenue, Winnipeg, MB Canada R3M 3S3

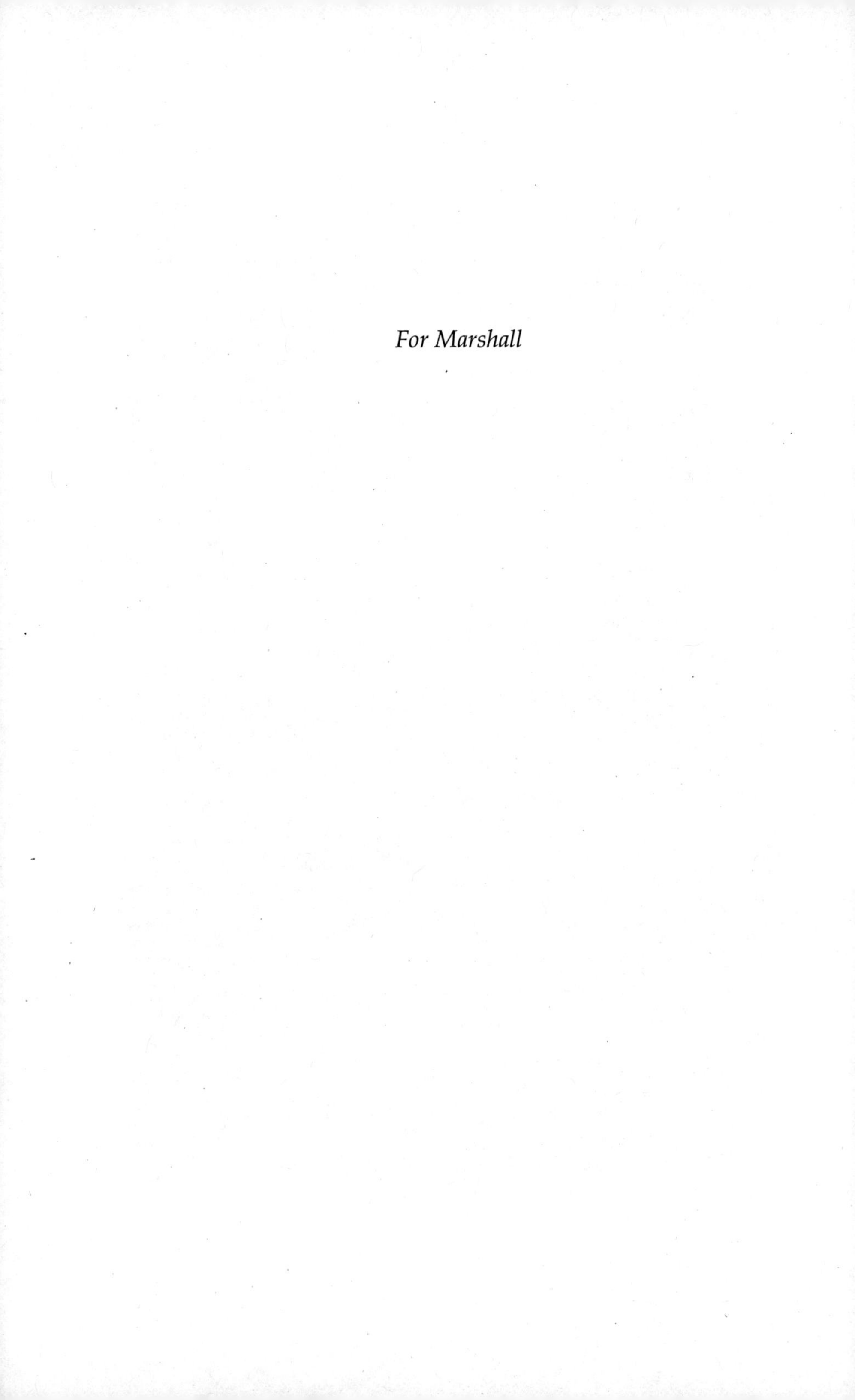

For Marshall

Corey Payette

Corey Payette is an interdisciplinary storyteller, writer, composer, producer, and director in theatre and film. He is a member of the Mattagami First Nations, with French Canadian and Irish ancestry, and lives on the unceded territories of the xʷməθkʷəy̓əm (Musqueam), Skwxwú7mesh (Squamish), and səl'ilwətaʔɬ (Tsleil-Waututh) peoples. Known for his deeply moving, large-scale original musical creations, Payette challenges the public's notion of what musicals can be, inserting Indigenous perspectives and narratives into mainstream spaces, igniting conversations that inspire social change. Payette's work explores themes of colonization, Indigenous language revitalization, cultural healing, reconciliation between Indigenous and non-Indigenous peoples, and the complexity of historic and contemporary Indigenous experiences across music, theatre, and film. His musicals include *Children of God*, *Les Filles du Roi*, and *Starwalker*. He is the recipient of the BC Reconciliation Award, the John Hirsch Prize, and a Fleck Fellowship, and he has won four Ovation Awards and two Jessie Awards.

www.coreypayette.com

Acknowledgements

Originally commissioned by The Musical Stage Company, Toronto ON, Mitchell Marcus, Artistic and Managing Director. Commissioned with funding from the Aubrey and Marla Dan Fund for New Musicals. Developed with The Musical Stage Co., Urban Ink and Raven Theatre with the support of The Cultch, Deer Lake Artist Retreat at the Shadbolt Centre for the Arts, National Arts Centre Indigenous Theatre, and Warner Media Access Canada Writer's Group.

Julie McIsaac, Marshall McMahen, Patrice Bowler, David Therriault, Ray Hogg, Aaron Willis, Jonathan Corkal, Cassandra Di Felice, Thom Allison, Dillan Chiblow, Aaron Hastelow, Bryan Hindle, Matt Nethersole, Jacob MacInnis, Tyler Pearse, Robert Ball, Landon Doak, Victoria Wang, Cheyenne Scott, Vanessa Sears, Melissa Tsang, Maria Zarrillo, Amy Cornish, Fabian Aspell Morales, Kamila Sediego, Ralph Escamillan and VanVogueJam.

Playwright's Notes

Starwalker began as a deeply personal exploration of my Two-Spirit identity and a love letter to my queer community in East Vancouver. I started writing this musical at a time when drag queen story hours weren't under attack, when the findings from the National Inquiry into Missing and Murdered Indigenous Women, Girls, and Two-Spirit People had not yet come to light, and when the fight for equality seemed to be making greater strides. But the world has shifted, and so has the urgency of *Starwalker*.

This musical is an act of joyful rebellion—a celebration of resilience and the enduring power of love. At its heart, *Starwalker* weaves together Indigenous culture and drag performance to shine a light on the vibrant, transformative power of unapologetic self-expression. It's a tribute to our families—both those we are born into and those we choose—to the beauty that exists within us all, and to the sacred, unshakable power that has always lived on this land.

My hope is that *Starwalker* will inspire audiences to see the world through a lens of love and possibility, and to celebrate the joy of being exactly who you were always meant to be.

Production History

Starwalker premiered February 16–March 5, 2023, a co-production by Urban Ink and Raven Theatre in association with The Musical Stage Co. and presented by The Cultch at the York Theatre, on the unceded territories of the xʷməθkʷəy̓əm (Musqueam), Skwxwú7mesh (Squamish), and səl'ilwəta?ł (Tsleil-Waututh) peoples in East Vancouver, British Columbia.

Cast

Starwalker	Dillan Chiblow
Mother	Stewart Adam McKensy
Levi	Jeffrey Follis
Michael	Jesse Alvarez
Sissy	Ryan Maschke
Cookie	Connor Parnall
Ensemble:	Ralph Escamillan and August Elzinga

Creative Team

Book/Music/Lyrics	Corey Payette
Directed	Corey Payette
Choreography	Ralph Escamillan
Music Direction	Sean Bayntun

Set Design: .... Anna Shearing

Costume Design: .... Alaia Hamer

Lighting Design: .... Jonathan Kim

Sound Design: ....Brad Danyluk

Producer: .... Fabian Aspell Morales

Assistant Choreographer: .... Ross Wirtanen

Fight Director: .... Mike Kovac

Intimacy Director: ....Lisa Goebel

Head of Wardrobe: ....Tiffany Bishop

Stage Manager: .... Melanie Thompson

Assistant Stage Manager: .... Sara Allison

Apprentice Stage Manager: .... Jennifer Wilson

Originally commissioned by The Musical Stage Company, Toronto ON, Mitchell Marcus, Artistic and Managing Director.

Commissioned with funding from the Aubrey and Marla Dan Fund for New Musicals.

Developed with The Musical Stage Co., Urban Ink and Raven Theatre, with the support of The Cultch, Deer Lake Artist Retreat, National Arts Centre Indigenous Theatre and Warner Media Access Canada Writers' Group.

Levi (Jeffrey Follis) puts Star (Dillan Chiblow) in drag for the first time. Photo by David Cooper Photography.

Star (Dillan Chiblow) performs in drag for the first time at the House of Borealis. Photo by David Cooper Photography.

The House of Borealis (Jesse Alvarez, Connor Parnall, Ryan Maschke, Jeffrey Follis, Dillan Chiblow, August Elzinga, & Ralph Escamillan) performs at the Winter Solstice Ball. Photo by David Cooper Photography.

The House of Borealis (Connor Parnall, Jeffrey Follis, Ralph Escamillan, Stewart Adam McKensy, August Elzinga, Jesse Alvarez, and Ryan Maschke) perform the opening number. Photo by David Cooper Photography.

Mother Borealis (Stewart Adam McKensy) introduces Star (Dillan Chiblow) for her first performance at the House of Borealis (Ryan Maschke and Ralph Escamillan opening curtain). Photo by David Cooper Photography.

Star (Dillan Chiblow) performing with the House of Borealis (Stewart Adam McKensy, Jeffrey Follis, Ryan Maschke, Jesse Alvarez, Connor Parnall, August Elzinga, Ralph Escamillan) in "Rebellion Song" that mixes drag and protest. Photo by David Cooper Photography.

Characters

Eddie Starwalker ("Star"): Mixed Oji-Cree heritage, late 20s, sweet but tough. Soft but hardened.

Levi Borealis: Late 20s, early 30s. Brooding, dark sense of humour, a sharp wit, funny, with a grounded spirit that stays in the room long after he's gone. Lives in the House of Borealis.

Mother Aurora Borealis: The mother of the House of Borealis. She is full of love and affection, but do not cross her.

Michael (aka "Cassie O'pea"): A seasoned Queen at the House of Borealis. Gives off major stage manager vibes and keeps everything running smoothly in the house.

Sissy Garçon: Mature. "The Art Queen." Takes herself way too seriously. Mother's closest confidant. Is the visual creative force of the House of Borealis, a master of constructing looks, and believes bright colours to be gaudy.

Cookie Von Herstenberg: Young. "The Reveal Queen." Addicted to speed, is the life of the party, and a bit of a mess.

Ensemble: Store clerk, Store manager, Queens, Paramedics.

All roles must be comfortable in drag.

Note: pronouns are used interchangeably throughout, with characters being referred to as "he/him", "she/her", and "they/them". Some characters are "he/him" out of drag, and "she/her" in drag, while others are "they/them" throughout.

Setting

Story takes place on the Unceded Territories of the xʷməθkʷəy̓əm (Musqueam), Skwxwú7mesh (Squamish), and səl'ilwətaʔɬ (Tsleil-Waututh) peoples known today as East Van Rez (East Vancouver).

Present day.

Songs

1. What They Don't Know About You ....All
2. Rebellion Song .... Starwalker
3. Strut That Ass, Honey ....Mother & All
4. In The Starlight.. Starwalker & Levi
5. Rules Of Passing.............................. Levi, Starwalker, & All
6. A Home For Those Who Had None .... Mother
7. God In Drag, You're Beautiful........Levi, Star, Mother, & All
8. Rebellion Song [Reprise]...............................Starwalker & All
9. Bothered .... Sissy, Michael, & Cookie
10. Something We Don't Know .... Michael, Sissy & Mother
11. When We Fall (Winter Solstice Ball) ....All
12. This Broken Mess ....Levi & All
13. Loved You Since The Day I Was Born .... Levi & Star
14. What They Don't Know About You [Reprise] ....Queens
15. In The Starlight [Reprise] .... Levi
16. Soar..Starwalker
17. Fancy Dance..Starwalker & All

Act One

Scene 1

> *In the House of Borealis. Darkness. There is a small stage set up in the middle of the room where MOTHER BOREALIS appears draped over a chair, gown dripping to the floor. The audience surrounds her, within reach.*

1. <u>WHAT THEY DON'T KNOW ABOUT YOU</u>

MOTHER: WHAT YOU SEE, WHAT YOU KNOW, ALL
THE PARTS WE'LL NEVER SHOW
THERE'S A PLACE WE CAN GO WHERE
YOU'LL BE THINKING OF ME
DOESN'T THAT SOUND SWEET
A PLACE THAT YOU WOULDN'T GO
IF ALL THE OTHERS COULD SEE

> *From the audience, a spotlight hits LEVI, who emerges and makes his way through the crowd, singing to the audience as he passes them.*

LEVI: YOU MAY LEARN TO BE SCARED
THAT NO ONE EVER HAS CARED
YOU MAY NOT BE WHAT THEY SEE
BUT ALL THEY SAY ISN'T TRUE
WHAT THEY DON'T KNOW ABOUT YOU
AND I CAN TELL YOU EACH TIME
WHAT THEY DON'T KNOW ABOUT YOU

MOTHER: DON'T TELL ME THE WAYS YOU WERE
              LOST AND FOUND YOUR WAY

LEVI: DON'T TELL ME 'CAUSE BAE BEING LOST
              IS REALLY MY THING
              AND THAT'S ME.

MOTHER: WANNA SEE?

              *MICHAEL emerges from behind the
              onstage curtains.*

MICHAEL: THEY MAY FREEZE, POINT AND STARE
              AS IF YOU EVER COULD CARE
              THEY DON'T SEE WHAT COULD BE
              WHEN THEY ARE LOOKING AT YOU
              AS IF THEIR FEARS HAVE COME TRUE
              COUNT ALL THE WAYS THAT THEY'RE
              BLIND
              WHAT THEY DON'T KNOW ABOUT YOU

MOTHER: DON'T TELL ME THE WAYS YOU WERE
              LOST AND FOUND YOUR WAY

LEVI &
MICHAEL: DON'T TELL ME 'CAUSE BAE BEING LOST
              IS REALLY MY THING
              AND THAT'S ME.

MOTHER: WANNA SEE?

              *SISSY and COOKIE enter from the
              audience and make their way to the stage.*

ALL: POSE, POSE, POSE
              AND HIT THE FLOOR
              POSE, POSE, POSE
              THEY'RE WANTING MORE
              GIVE A POSE, POSE, POSE

REACH FOR THE SKY
THAT POSE, POSE, POSE
WILL GIVE THEM LIFE

> *All the QUEENS strike a pose and snap their fingers.*

THAT POSE
THAT POSE
THAT POSE
THAT POSE!

MICHAEL: Welcome to the House of Borealis! Here's Sissy Garçon, "The Art Queen." And Cookie, "The Reveal Queen." And I'm Cassie O'Pea, your host for this evening. We stand on the shoulders of greatness. In solidarity with the Indigenous peoples on whose land this house is based, hunny. No touching the Queens. Hands off the merchandise. But do tip the dawls. Now, the one legendary Queen who needs no introduction, the mother of this house, the twinkle in your eye, the trip in your step, giving you that night you'll never forget—"Mother Borealis"!

> *MOTHER BOREALIS walks out on the runway and takes everyone's breath away. The audience is so excited to see her, and her energy is infectious.*

MOTHER: Welcome, ladies and... well... gender's a spectrum, and we're all stars at the House of Borealis! Your one-stop shop for everything tucked, plucked, and a little bit fucked okay. We have a special performance for you here tonight, Clown Town Couture, Jizzney Princess, and our best drag, Eleganza Extravaganza. There is no fan favourite, this is not a democracy, no mail-in voting here, it is up to the judges to decide—oh wait, that's me! Remember hunny, it's not that serious, it's just drag. Do we want to have a good time tonight? Oh my god, Cassie, hunny, I think these people have fallen asleep. I said, "Do we wanna have a good time tonight?" That's more like it! Now hold on to your hairpieces and let's get to werk!

> *Backstage, while all the action is happening onstage, LEVI is putting on his jacket and hat getting ready to go out. MICHAEL is back there putting some powder on her forehead, dressed in angel cherub drag.*

MICHAEL: Oh, they're eating it up tonight!

LEVI: They always do.

MICHAEL: Where are you off to mid-show?

LEVI: I'm only in the opening number tonight. So I'm heading out for… an actual walk.

MICHAEL: An actual walk. Right, like anyone has gone for a "walk" at this hour. You're going to hook up!

LEVI: Want me to bring you back some?

MICHAEL: Don't toy with me in a tuck or I'll tear my tights.

LEVI: More for me.

> *LEVI kisses MICHAEL, grabs a candy from her bowl, and bounces out the door, smiling wide.*

MICHAEL: Uh, he keeps me young.

> *Back onstage to the performance.*

ALL: THAT POSE, POSE, POSE
AND HIT THE FLOOR
THAT POSE, POSE, POSE
THEY'RE WANTING MORE
GIVE A POSE, POSE, POSE
REACH FOR THE SKY
THAT POSE, POSE, POSE
WILL GIVE THEM LIFE

THAT POSE
THAT POSE
THAT POSE
OF THEM WILL GIVE YOU LIFE
OH YEAH

Scene 2

In the park, EDDIE STARWALKER "STAR," is sitting under a big willow tree. It is night and dark in the park, except for a lamp light above the park bench.

2. REBELLION SONG

STAR: WAY HI YEAH HI WAY HI YO
WAY HI YEAH HI WAY HI YO
WAY HI WAY HI WAY HI YO
WAY HI WAY HI WAY HI YO

WHERE'S HIS MOTHER, WHERE'D SHE GO?
WHERE'S HIS FATHER, DOES HE KNOW?
WAY HI WAY HI AND SO IT GOES
WAY HI WAY HI JUST SO YOU KNOW

GO TO CLASS, THEY ALL WOULD SAY
DON'T BE AN ASS YOU'LL LOSE YOUR WAY
WAY HI WAY HI TOOK ME AWAY
WAY HI WAY HI TO A WHITE MAN'S I STAY

LEFT THERE BATTERED, BEATEN, BRUISED
LEFT THERE KNOWING LOVE AS ABUSE
WAY HI WAY HI RUN AS FAST AS YOU CAN
WAY HI WAY HI THEY'LL NEVER TAKE YOU AGAIN

I WANT MORE THAN THEY EXPECT OF ME
I WANT A HOME WHERE IT'S SAFE TO BE
WAY HI WAY HI WILL I FIND IT AGAIN?
WAY HI WAY HI IF NOT NOW THEN WHEN?

WAY HI YEAH HI WAY HI YO
WAY HI YEAH HI WAY HI YO
WAY HI WAY HI WAY HI YO
WAY HI WAY HI WAY HI YO

WAY HI YEAH HI WAY HI YO
WAY HI YEAH HI WAY HI YO
WAY HI WAY HI WAY HI YO
WAY HI WAY HI WAY HI YO

LEVI approaches, sits on the opposite side of the tree, out of view of STAR. A MAN walks by with a baseball hat on, hiding his face; he's a tall, attractive man. He stops near the park bench to tie his shoe, catches LEVI looking at him, but also sees STAR from the other side of the tree. Both men think that the MAN in the baseball hat is looking at them. They both stand up as he walks down the path toward them, eyeing them up, until they step forward from the cover of the tree and are startled to see each other. The MAN walks down the trail, looking back to see which of them is going to follow him.

LEVI: Oh my God, you scared the shit out of me.

STAR: How long have you been hiding there?

LEVI: I wasn't hiding. And trust, he was looking at you.

STAR: How do you know that?

LEVI: I get a hunch when someone is eyeing me up or not.

STAR: A hunch.

LEVI: It's a gift.

STAR: Well, that gift let a trick get away.

LEVI: Chase him down. I bet it would have been fun.

STAR: You have lots of those experiences?

LEVI: Every now and then.

STAR: If the money's right.

LEVI: Guys like you are turning tricks now? No wonder my johns are drying up.

STAR: I use Grindr mostly. This isn't my turf or anything.

LEVI: She's a businessman.

STAR: It's a living.

STAR starts to leave.

LEVI: My name's Levi.

STAR: Eddie. But my friends call me Star.

They give a wave and a smile and get a bit embarrassed. They laugh.

What?

LEVI: No, it's nothing. I just… I live at the House of Borealis—it's a drag house… like a club… You ever watch *Drag Race*?

STAR: I've heard of it. Never seen it.

LEVI: Have you been living under a rock?

STAR: No, just living out here.

LEVI: Well, Mother bought the House of Borealis back when buying a house in East Van was something a normal person could do…

STAR: What's a borealis…

LEVI: Borealis is like the colours in the sky.

STAR: Oh…like northern lights.

LEVI: Yeah. Mother would lose her shit if she met someone named Star. She's superstitious like that.

STAR: Like men dressing up like women?

LEVI: Why? Does that freak you out?

STAR: No, just making sure we are on the same page.

LEVI: Well, it is so much more than that. How about people dressing up as the illusion of gender, poking fun at stereotypes, and saying "fuck you" to the ways we're told we need to live. But way more fabulous. It is really creative, if you're into that sort of thing.

STAR: Yeah, I am, sort of? Anyways… I'll catch you around sometime. Levi, right?

STAR starts to leave.

LEVI: Yeah, Star… *(Pause.)* You know, I figured tough trade on the street wouldn't be into the glamour I'm talking about.

STAR: You don't know anything about me.

LEVI: A hunch, remember?

STAR: I dressed in my ma's high heels when I was a kid too, you know.

LEVI: Oh! Now we're talkin'! So when are you gonna come check us out?

STAR: I usually spend these hours of the night walking around until the sun comes up…

LEVI: …So real busy then…

STAR: Okay, okay, I'll come check it out sometime.

LEVI: There's actually a show happening right now.

STAR: Is this some sort of elaborate act to get me to go home with you?

LEVI: It's not an act. This is the real thing, honey!

LEVI grabs STAR's hand and they run down the park path towards the street.

Scene 3

> *Back at the House of Borealis, LEVI and STAR enter the dimly lit club space just as the second category is happening. The category is "Clown Town Couture," and all the QUEENS are dressed in their favourite high-fashion clown attire. MOTHER BOREALIS is seated in a large chair watching the QUEENS perform for her. The audience is cheering as LEVI and STAR make their way through the crowd.*

3. STRUT THAT ASS, HONEY

ALL:

STRUT THAT ASS, HONEY
MAKE THEM GAG UPON IT
BILLS RAIN, KEEP 'EM COMING
MAKE IT LAST FOREVER

SISSY:

DID YOU SEE HER?
WANT TO BE HER?
WAIT TO READ HER
CAUSE WE DON'T GIVE A FUCK IF SHE'S A DIVA

MICHAEL:

GLUE THAT LACE FRONT
CINCH THAT WAIST, HUN
WORK A CHEAP STUNT
DON'T GIVE THE TIME A DAY TO A DIVA

ALL:

STRUT THAT ASS, HONEY
MAKE THEM GAG UPON IT
BILLS RAIN, KEEP 'EM COMING
MAKE IT LAST FOREVER

> *During the performance, MICHAEL finds LEVI in the crowd.*

MICHAEL: Levi, thank Jebus Crabs you're back. Cookie has locked herself in the bathroom, we need you to go on for her in the second category. Come on.

LEVI: Can't you see I'm busy?

               MICHAEL shoots a look to STAR and back to LEVI.

MICHAEL: Trick or treat?

LEVI: Treat.

MICHAEL: Great, he can stay here and watch.

LEVI: No.

MICHAEL: Levi, look at me. This glitter is layered on thick. There's no way I can pull off a Cookie Von Herstenberg reveal after living my Precious Moments fantasy.

LEVI: Fine. *(To STAR.)* Are you okay here?

STAR: I might take off.

LEVI: No, I'm going to go on in a bit. Stay if you want to see me up there. It's the Jizzney Princess category, if you're into that.

STAR: Okay. I'll stay.

LEVI: Good.

               They smile. MICHAEL is impatient. They snap out of it and LEVI starts to go through the crowd.

MICHAEL: Okay, enough with the foreplay.

LEVI: *(To STAR.)* I'll see you after.

LEVI makes his way backstage with MICHAEL, and STAR finds a spot closer to the front of the crowd to better watch the action. He finds the best view of the stage, almost like the whole show is being done for him.

MOTHER: ARE YOU NEW HERE?
YOU A GOOD QUEER?
TO BE SEEN HERE
YOU NEED TO TURN THE LEVEL UP TO DIVA

GIVE GOOD FACE, HONEY
HUSTLING'S GOOD MONEY
NO COMPLAINTS TO MOMMY
IF YOU REALLY ASPIRE TO BE SOMEBODY

ALL: STRUT THAT ASS, HONEY
MAKE THEM GAG UPON IT
BILLS RAIN, KEEP 'EM COMING
MAKE IT LAST FOREVER

BUTCH QUEENS NOT WANTED
SERVE THEM FACE FOREVER
CAKE SMACKS SHABLAM FLAT
ALWAYS BRINGS THE HOUSE DOWN

The category ends and then it is LEVI's group. STAR is looking around, noticing how the atmosphere in the place is changing; people are excited for this group. A dream sequence launches, where the QUEENS onstage all seem to focus on STAR in the audience.

SISSY: WHO'S THAT WITH HER?

MICHAEL: HE'S A DRIFTER…

SISSY: IT'S SO LIKE HER

<table>
<tr><td></td><td>TO DISAPPEAR WITHOUT A WAY TO
REACH HER</td></tr>
<tr><td>MICHAEL:</td><td>SAID IT WOULD BE FUN</td></tr>
<tr><td>SISSY:</td><td>SAY YES AND PLAY DUMB
ONLY THIS ONCE
IT WOULD BE A MATTER OF TIME BEFORE
THEY TOOK ONE</td></tr>
<tr><td>MOTHER</td><td>NOT WORTH THE MONEY
TOOK MORE THAN THEY PAID FOR
NECK CHOKED, FACE BLOODY</td></tr>
<tr><td>SISSY:</td><td>PLEASE DON'T LAST FOREVER
DON'T LAST FOREVER</td></tr>
</table>

The dream sequence breaks and we're back in the heightened energy of the club. LEVI and another QUEEN enter the battle area as dance music begins. LEVI is wearing his Belle outfit that reveals into Beast pants. The audience can't take their eyes off him; he's perfect in every way. As LEVI takes centre stage, he shoots a look at STAR standing on the other side of the room and gives a smile. Then puts on his game face, and fiercely works his outfit with so much power and presence. They're dancing up a storm with the audience going wild for him.

<table>
<tr><td>ALL:</td><td>GLUE THAT LACE FRONT
CINCH THAT WAIST, HUN
WORK A CHEAP STUNT
DON'T GIVE THE TIME A DAY TO A DIVA

STRUT THAT ASS, HONEY
MAKE THEM GAG UPON IT
BILLS RAIN, KEEP 'EM COMING
MAKE IT LAST FOREVER</td></tr>
</table>

STRUT THAT ASS, HONEY
MAKE THEM GAG UPON IT
BILLS RAIN, KEEP 'EM COMING
MAKE IT LAST FOREVER
MAKE IT LAST FOREVER

> *The crowd erupts in applause for the QUEENS. LEVI scores tens across the board from MOTHER and wins the category. STAR is now celebrating with strangers in the crowd with no idea what this means.*

Scene 4

> *In the QUEENS' dressing room, an upper room in the house, not a theatre dressing room or anything fancy. There are outfits everywhere, sewing machines, fabric, hats, wigs, completely covering the entire room. LEVI is taking off his makeup and outfit. Outside the door there's some sort of ruckus happening in the hallway. There's a banging at the door; MICHAEL opens the door a crack, and a booming voice comes through.*

MICHAEL: Don't be that girl.

COOKIE: Excuse me, I'm just wanting to talk to her.

MICHAEL: No, go back downstairs.

LEVI: It was supposed to be my night off.

COOKIE: Why won't you let me in?

MICHAEL: Take your drama someplace else.

LEVI: I didn't even want to go on.

               MICHAEL waves STAR in from the hallway, and they sneak into the dressing room.

COOKIE: I'm just saying I coulda performed if…

MICHAEL: *(To STAR.)* Come in.

LEVI: …you hadn't been passed out?

               COOKIE in the hall is trying to restrain STAR from behind.

STAR: Get your hands off me!

LEVI: He's with me!

STAR: Yeah, I'm with him! *(To LEVI.)* Thanks!

COOKIE: I was resting my eyes!

               MICHAEL pushes COOKIE out of the dressing room and shuts the door giving a dirty look back at STAR.

LEVI: Can you believe her? Try to help people.

STAR: I have no words for what I just saw.

LEVI: You like?

STAR: I was not prepared for that.

LEVI: And you weren't all weirded out by the boy you met passing so well as a beast?

STAR: I couldn't take my eyes off of you.

LEVI: Good, that's the idea.

STAR: How long have you been doing this?

LEVI: Since I was fourteen. I was a baby when I started.

STAR: And you won!

LEVI: The shows are framed as competitions, but we know who wins. It's how we make our money.

STAR: Oh. Are you always performing here?

LEVI: We sometimes do bigger gigs in fancy theatres, but this is our usual spot. Gotta keep the regulars happy.

STAR: I've never seen that much money!

LEVI: That's what pays the rent, and then we split the rest.

STAR: Is there room for a 'nishinabe princess?

LEVI: What? Really? Well, you'll have to meet Mama.

They exit the dressing room and rush down the hall to MOTHER's room. QUEENS are passing them carrying costumes and wigs.

Scene 5

In MOTHER's room on the top floor of the house. LEVI knocks on the door. SISSY is next to MOTHER at the dressing table.

LEVI: Mama, it's Levi.

MOTHER: Yes, baby.

They enter MOTHER's room.

LEVI: I have someone I wanted to introduce you to.

MOTHER: Don't you be bringing no trick home to me.

LEVI: He's not a trick. He came to watch us perform tonight. Thought he could stay?

MOTHER: And where did you meet this boy?

LEVI: That doesn't matter, but a very respectable place.

SISSY: Lees Trail busy at this hour?

LEVI: Shut up, Siss.

SISSY: I call it like I see it.

MOTHER: Bring me the child.

LEVI: *(To STAR.)* Don't worry. She's all bark.

STAR: Aanii… I mean hello.

            STAR puts out his hand to shake MOTHER's, but she puts out her hand for him to kiss it. He does.

MOTHER: Charmed.

STAR: That was amazing tonight.

MOTHER: My children rocked it, again. I keep telling them they're great, but they won't believe me. Maybe they'll take it from you.

SISSY: Cookie is all theatrics, she coulda dragged herself on stage if she wanted to. I saw her perform once with a chuck bucket in the wings.

LEVI: You're lucky I happened to be here to save your ass.

SISSY: You're so full of yourself.

LEVI: Full of body-ody-ody.

STAR: *(To MOTHER.)* What does it take to do something like that?

MOTHER: An intricate web of duct tape and fishing wire.

STAR: Wow.

MOTHER: Always nice to still be able to impress the youths.

LEVI: His name is Star. I figured she might be a good fit for the House of Borealis.

MOTHER: You already have a borealis name… how did you manage that?

STAR: My name is actually Eddie Starwalker but everyone calls me Star.

MOTHER: J'approve. Do you know where it is from?

STAR: Mama gave it to me as a nickname from a Buffy song. It was my parents' favourite, every time it came on the radio. Guess they thought it sounded like me, or something.

SISSY: I wouldn't have guessed you were Native.

STAR: Well, I am. Oji-Cree.

MOTHER: Oji…who? What is that?

STAR: It's the land where my family is from. But it's no big deal. I don't know much about it… any of it. I didn't grow up with it. So… why do you call it the House of Borealis?

MOTHER: Because we are what…

ALL: Out of this world, hunny!

SISSY: Too bad we already have a houseful.

MOTHER: Sissy's right. And I'm not about to put any young thing on my stage. These people pay good money for the Borealis Experience.

LEVI: Come on! I was rough when I started, too.

SISSY: He hasn't even been in drag yet. Quit pushing this so hard. The Motha has spoken.

LEVI: This is bullshit.

STAR: It's fine, Levi.

LEVI: *(To STAR.)* No, no it is not fine. *(To SISSY.)* After all I've put into this house—I saved your ass tonight while Cookie was in a fit. I didn't have to do that!

SISSY: Oh, here we go! I guess Cookie isn't the only one with theatrics.

LEVI: Next time you need saving, don't come looking for me.

SISSY: Oh, hunny, trust me. No one is looking for you!

MOTHER: Hold on!

            MOTHER stands and immediately starts coughing and needing to sit back down again. Everyone is in silence watching her.

            You're all exhausting me with this. The first question is: Star, are you actually wanting to do drag?

STAR: I don't know yet.

MOTHER: With cheekbones like that, you can pull off any look. Are you a thief?

STAR shakes his head no.

(*To LEVI.*) Aww, he's a liar… and sweet. (*To STAR.*) You aren't going to hurt anybody, right?

STAR shakes his head no.

Good. Well, that's a start. You can stay here tonight. But unless you are going to perform, I don't know what to do with you.

LEVI: Let me help him put a look together for you.

MOTHER: All right, I already said he could stay the night. What more do you want from me?

LEVI: Thanks, Mama.

LEVI gives MOTHER a kiss. He leads STAR out of the room.

Scene 6

LEVI and STAR come outside onto the steps of the House of Borealis. It is so late it is almost morning.

LEVI: I figured by the time I walked out onstage you'd take one look at me and run for the door.

STAR: I prepared myself for it not to be great.

LEVI: Oh yeah?

STAR: So when you came out looking half-decent, I was pleasantly surprised.

LEVI: Half-decent? How dare you? Reading me on your first night at a ball.

STAR: Reading? What is that?

LEVI: Like insulting someone or judging them but with a bit of sass.

STAR: I guess I picked it up fast.

LEVI: What was your favourite part?

STAR: I think it was the one who came out with the disco ball on her head. She had the right attitude.

LEVI: Okay, I guess I see that.

STAR: Are you reading my choices?

LEVI: No, it's just you can learn a lot about a person by what drag they're into.

STAR: Okay, then… what does it say about me?

LEVI: That you like balls on your head.

They laugh.

STAR: You didn't need to search too hard to figure that out.

LEVI: So would you ever do it?

STAR: Put balls on my head?

LEVI: No, get in drag?

STAR: It looks like a lot of money to put all that together. I don't have anything like that.

LEVI: That's why you join the House of Borealis. We'll hook you up.

STAR: Really?

LEVI: Yes, Mary. You think I have the money to buy all this shit? We buy one garment, pass it along, sew it together, and glue it on. And then you can be part of the house. We make art, share it, and pass it along to the next person. We're like a little bohemian family.

STAR: You're a family.

4. IN THE STARLIGHT

LEVI: Well yeah, that's what comes with living in the house.

STAR: Right…

LEVI: Is there something wrong?

STAR: No, I should go.

LEVI: Don't go. Mother said you could stay with us.

STAR starts to leave, but LEVI stops him.

STAR: THERE'VE BEEN MANY OTHER BOYS BEFORE, BOYS BEFORE YOU.
THEY HAVE NEVER WANTED THAT MUCH MORE THAN I GAVE
ALL I COULD GIVE WAS ONLY A NIGHT OR TWO AT MOST

FOR A TIME I THOUGHT OF NOTHING MORE, IT'S SHALLOW
I'D SNEAK OUT EVERY NIGHT AND SLEEP ALL THROUGH THE DAY
THERE'D BE A DIFFERENT GUY WITH ME, NOT KNOWING HIS NAME

IN THE STARLIGHT, OF MOONLIGHT, WHEN THE TIME'S RIGHT—I NEVER FEEL ALONE
I FALL AWAY WITH HIM

I STUMBLE HOME WITH HIM
A THOUSAND BEDS I'M IN
AND NOT RETURN
I'M CALLING OUT TO HIM
I'M CRAWLING BACK TO HIM
BUT NO SOUND COMES OUT OF MY
MOUTH

ARE YOU ONE OF ALL THOSE BOYS
BEFORE?
IT'S OKAY IF YOU ARE.
I'M NOT TRYING TO FREAK YOU OUT OR
ANYTHING LIKE THAT
BUT IF YOU HAD A GOOD FEELING,
TOO...
MAYBE I COULD GET INTO THAT WITH
YOU?
IT'S NOT SOMETHING I WOULD USUALLY
DO, BUT WOULD YOU?

>*LEVI leans in and gives STAR a very innocent kiss and they both smile.*

STAR: I guess that's a yes.

LEVI: It's not a no.

>*STAR turns around and starts to go.*

Say a boy wanted to meet up with another boy. Where would he find him?

STAR: I know where you live, remember? I'll find you.

LEVI: Madame.

STAR: Good lady.

>*STAR curtsies and LEVI gets up and goes in the front door. LEVI goes into the house.*

STAR: ALL THIS TIME WITH HIM AND I WANT
MORE, A STRANGE FEELING
THESE HOURS SPENT WITH HIM FEEL
LIKE FOREVER AND A DAY
THESE HOURS SPENT WITH HIM BUT
PLEASE DON'T LET THEM FADE AWAY

IN THE STARLIGHT, OF MOONLIGHT,
IS THE TIME RIGHT? I'LL NEVER BE THE
SAME.
I HAVE FALLEN INTO HIM
WORDS STUMBLE OUT WITH HIM
A THOUSAND BEDS I'VE BEEN IN
BUT NONE WITH HIM
I'M BUZZING FROM WITHIN
LET BUTTERFLIES GIVE IN
AND I'LL NEVER COME BACK DOWN
IF I WAS LOST THEN NOW I'M FOUND
TAKE THE WORLD I HAD BEFORE AND
GIVE ME MORE
IN THE STARLIGHT

STAR makes his way down the street as the sun starts to come up.

Scene 7

A week later, in a fancy department store changeroom, STAR and LEVI are shopping for clothes—and on a first date on the down-low. LEVI is in the changeroom. STAR enters, pretending to work at the store, and knocks.

STAR: How's that fitting? Can I get you another size or colour? Cinch you in? Tell me what you need, hunny?

LEVI flings open the changeroom curtain, revealing a beautiful summer dress paired with a large hat, sunglasses, and dangly pendant accessories.

LEVI: She's got the lingo already.

STAR: Hoooolllleehhhhhh! You look great!

LEVI: Oh, bless. The back is a cry for help, will it do up?

STAR: Yeah, let me see.

LEVI: It fits, that's all I need to know.

LEVI goes back into the changeroom.

This is a part of the process that is the worst. There's always some store clerk who makes it their business to say, "Did you know that's a women's dress?" as if I don't know that already.

LEVI comes back out fully dressed in their own clothes with the dress mixed in with a few male items.

Let's go.

5. RULES OF PASSING

LEVI: *(To STORE CLERK.)* Hi!

STORE CLERK: Did you find everything you needed today?

LEVI: Yep, we sure did.

The STORE CLERK rings up the items. LEVI looks around awkwardly and makes an "it's okay" face to STAR. Then hands the STORE CLERK a stack of cash.

STORE CLERK: Have a nice day!

> *STAR and LEVI leave the store.*

LEVI: (*To STAR.*) Did you see how she looked at me...? What a bitch.

> *They exit the store and run down the street laughing. In a second department store changeroom, STAR is now the one trying on the clothes. LEVI is waiting impatiently outside, looking through all the dresses STAR has chosen to try on. LEVI sings to himself.*

LEVI: RED, RED, RED, BLUE, RED
I GUESS HE MUST LIKE RED
WHAT'S THIS A SHAPELY SILHOUETTE
THAT'LL MAKE THEM ALL DROP DEAD
YOU KNOW THAT MOST OF THESE DETAILS
AREN'T VISIBLE FROM THE STAGE
AND YOU DON'T WEAR THIS UNLESS
YOU'RE TRYING TO HIDE YOUR AGE.

HOW WOULD YOU HAVE SURVIVED
WITHOUT ME BY YOUR SIDE
IT DOESN'T MATTER HOW HARD YOU TRY
IF YOU DON'T KNOW THE RULES OF PASSING
YOU'LL BE PASSED BY
YOU'LL BE PASSED BY

LEVI: Oh my gawd, it is like you've never tried on women's clothes before.

STAR: It is not that, but it is so delicate, and I don't want to rip it.

LEVI: Who cares if it rips... suck it in!

STAR: Someone made this, I want to respect that.

LEVI: You are too much, really.

             RIP, RIP, RIP, STITCH IT
             WE'LL TEACH YOU HOW TO SEW
             AND YOU'LL SEE ALL OF THIS FABRIC
             AS GARMENTS YOU CAN MOULD
             IT'S ALL THE LITTLE DETAILS PASSED
             DOWN
             FROM QUEENS BEFORE
             IT'S LIKE A GOWN THAT'S GIFTED
             DOWN FROM DRAG OF LORE

             HOW WOULD YOU HAVE SURVIVED
             WITHOUT ME BY YOUR SIDE
             IT DOESN'T MATTER HOW HARD YOU
             TRY
             IF YOU DON'T KNOW THE RULES OF
             PASSING
             YOU'LL BE PASSED BY
             YOU'LL BE PASSED BY

             *STAR pokes their head outside the curtain
             of the dressing room.*

STAR: Pssst… is the coast clear?

LEVI: No one will witness your chicken legs, now
             get out here!

             *STAR slowly opens the curtain and adjusts
             the dress. It is floor-length and is much
             more "pageant" than the sexy, flirty dresses
             of the nightclub.*

             Wow! Bae.

STAR: What?

LEVI: You look so good.

STAR:

There's some sort of wire jabbing me in the back.

LEVI:

Pain in the name of beauty, darling. Get used to it.

STAR gets a glimpse of the dress in the mirror and pauses for a moment. STAR sings to themself.

STAR:

PERHAPS IT WAS THE DRESS
THAT GLIMMERS IN THE LIGHT
PERHAPS IT WAS THE WAY
I KNEW IT AT THE SIGHT

AND NOW I KNOW THERE'S SOMETHING
IN IT THAT FEELS RIGHT
AND NOW I KNOW I MIGHT BE
WEARING THIS TONIGHT

HOW WOULD I HAVE SURVIVED
WITHOUT HIM BY MY SIDE
IT DOESN'T MATTER HOW HARD I TRY
IF I DON'T KNOW THE RULES OF PASSING
I'LL BE PASSED BY
I'LL BE PASSED BY

STAR's private moment breaks.

Huh…

LEVI:

Awww… Baby's first time in a dress.

STAR:

It is not. I just have never worn something like this before.

LEVI:

Listen, I totally get it. Same thing happened to me the first time. I started crying, it was a whole scene. I needed to be sedated.

STAR:

I'm giving you Two-Spirit realness.

> *LEVI kneels down to examine any alterations that would need to be made to the dress.*

LEVI: Two-Spirit — like two-faced or something?

STAR: I thought that too when I was a kid, thinking people were teasing me and calling me fake, you know? But Two-Spirit, from what I know, means that you have both masc and fem spirits inside you.

LEVI: Werk that boots the house down multi-spirit queen realness then!

STAR: Ahhh, did you see the price of this one? Two hundred dollars!

LEVI: And we'll return it as soon as we've copied the pattern and done, like, three to five numbers in it, don't worry.

STAR: I just don't think I've ever had something worth this much on my body before. It is a new experience for me, that's all.

LEVI: The novelty will fade, and you'll be counting down the minutes till you can tear it off.

STAR: How do you think I'd do onstage?

LEVI: Well, you still look like a man in a dress, so there's work to do, but it's not like it needs major adjustments. Now you just need to think about—what kind of woman would wear this kind of dress?

STAR: A rich one.

LEVI: Good. That's a start. But what kind of rich? There are many kinds. The realness is in the details.

STAR: Like a rich bitch. Judy, get me my pearls!

LEVI: I like it. But who is Judy, and why does she have your pearls?

STAR: I don't know, I heard it in an old movie when I was young. Sounded like a rich bitch thing to say.

LEVI: I love that Judy is incompetent and that you've clearly been waiting forever for these pearls.

STAR: Get it together, Judy! We took her in off the street and this is what we get, poor thing.

LEVI: Now your turn to deal with this clerk.

STAR: I got this.

STAR gives a bunch of their clothes to the STORE MANAGER, who looks them up and down but doesn't say a word.

STORE
MANAGER: You took your time in that changing room. Did you find everything you were looking for?

STAR: A DRESS! I'm buying a dress, and it looks great on me.

STORE
MANAGER: Great.

LEVI puts his head in his hands awkwardly as STAR gives the STORE MANAGER a rolled-up bunch of bills. They leave the store, crashing into mannequins along the way.

ALL: RED, RED, RED, BLUE, RED
I GUESS HE MUST LIKE RED

WHAT'S THIS—A SHAPELY SILHOUETTE
THAT'LL MAKE THEM ALL DROP DEAD
YOU KNOW THAT MOST OF THESE
DETAILS
AREN'T VISIBLE FROM THE STAGE
AND YOU DON'T WEAR THIS UNLESS
YOU'RE TRYING TO HIDE YOUR AGE.

HOW WOULD YOU HAVE SURVIVED
WITHOUT ME BY YOUR SIDE
IT DOESN'T MATTER HOW HARD YOU
TRY
IF YOU DON'T KNOW THE RULES OF
PASSING
YOU'LL BE PASSED BY
YOU'LL BE PASSED BY

(ROUND 2)   RIP, RIP, RIP, STITCH IT
WE'LL TEACH YOU HOW TO SEW
AND YOU'LL SEE ALL OF THIS FABRIC
AS GARMENTS YOU CAN MOULD
IT'S ALL THE LITTLE DETAILS PASSED
DOWN
FROM QUEENS BEFORE
IT'S LIKE A GOWN THAT'S GIFTED
DOWN FROM DRAG OF LORE

HOW WOULD YOU HAVE SURVIVED
WITHOUT ME BY YOUR SIDE
IT DOESN'T MATTER HOW HARD YOU
TRY
IF YOU DON'T KNOW THE RULES OF
PASSING
YOU'LL BE PASSED BY
YOU'LL BE PASSED BY

(ROUND 3) PERHAPS IT WAS THE DRESS
THAT GLIMMERS IN THE LIGHT
PERHAPS IT WAS THE WAY
I KNEW IT AT THE SIGHT

AND NOW I KNOW THERE'S SOMETHING
IN IT THAT FEELS RIGHT
AND NOW I KNOW I MIGHT BE
WEARING THIS TONIGHT

HOW WOULD I HAVE SURVIVED
WITHOUT HIM BY MY SIDE
IT DOESN'T MATTER HOW HARD I TRY
IF I DON'T KNOW THE RULES OF PASSING
I'LL BE PASSED BY
I'LL BE PASSED BY

Over the course of these rounds, STAR is given a few dance steps with a QUEEN but almost falls over, then is reluctantly taught to sew by SISSY but is terrible at it. After a bit of a montage of getting frustrated and giving up, STAR starts to pick up the steps and builds confidence in the dance. Finally, STAR holds up a dress that she's hemmed.

ALL: PERHAPS IT WAS THE DRESS

Scene 8

In MOTHER's room. MOTHER is getting dressed up, and STAR is looking through her racks of clothes. STAR pulls out a large sequined Las Vegas style showgirl's headpiece.

STAR: What is this?

MOTHER: We had a Vegas showgirl number a couple of years ago. I was going to get rid of it a while back. Must have ended up in the wormhole that is my closet.

STAR: I keep finding little random things that… for me, remind me of home. But if you were to look at them closely, they're all made for hippie women. I don't care though, for me, it gives me something, you know.

MOTHER: If it gives you that special feeling, you should wear it.

STAR: It even goes with the dress I bought the other day.

MOTHER: Ugh, say no more. It's a sign. What are you? Leo, Gemini? Star… that must be a summer birth?

STAR: I was born in…

MOTHER: No, don't tell me! This is what I'm known for. Do you think you just stumbled on the House of Borealis with that name and that beautiful face by chance? No! Way! It was fate.

STAR: Capri—

MOTHER: —corn. See! I knew it. Winter child. Just as I thought. This explains everything.

STAR: Does it explain my fucked-up childhood?

MOTHER: No, afraid not.

STAR: Before I came here. I looked up to the stars, trying to find the bear.

MOTHER: Ursa Major.

STAR: Yeah, it's super major. It looks like a bear, there are shapes of it in the stars.

MOTHER: Oh my god, I love you.

STAR: No, I'm serious. And when I look up and can find it, I know that points east.

MOTHER: Why do you need to know where east is?

STAR: Because that's the way home. At least for me.

MOTHER   That gave me chills, you little fucker.

6. A HOME FOR THOSE WHO HAD NONE

STAR: My father taught me about the stars before I was taken away. He told me how to find my way home if I ever got lost. I sometimes wonder if it would work now. Years later. If I just followed those same stars east toward the bear? If I'd stumble upon my family again? Maybe they're stumbling toward me, and we'll just crash into each other one day. Like fate.

MOTHER: Why don't you stay in touch?

STAR: I would, if I could—that's what's fucked-up about being taken away and put in care, they don't put you back or connect you if you run away from that foster family.

MOTHER: I KNOW THE PAST HURTS
              IT COMES IN FAST BURSTS
              DON'T LET THAT VOICE GUIDE YOU
              IT'S NOT THE ONLY THING INSIDE YOU

STAR: Easy to say when you know exactly who you are and have a place like this to call home.

MOTHER: It wasn't that straightforward.

STAR: You're telling me there's more hidden back there in that closet?

MOTHER: More than you know.

STAR: I'm not one to judge anyone. Has this always been your family?

MOTHER: I CAME FROM A LIFE YOU'VE NEVER KNOWN
               I HAD A WIFE, TWO SONS NOW GROWN
               SPINNING INSIDE AN ENDLESS LOOP
               NOT KNOWING A WAY TO BREAK THROUGH UNTIL

               I'D SNEAK OUT WEEKNIGHTS
               I LIVED A DOUBLE LIFE
               THE SECRECY ENTICED ME
               A DARKNESS BURNED
               BUT THEN SHE FOUND ME THERE

               MY WIFE WAS STANDING AT THE DOOR
               "WHY? YOU LIAR!"
               SHE ASKED ME HOW LONG I HAD KNOWN
               SHE TOOK MY BOYS, THEIR FATHER'S GONE
               SHE LEFT ME ALL, ALL ALONE

MOTHER: Their mother doesn't let them see me. She thinks that I run a brothel or something. I wonder what gave her that idea?

STAR: Do you miss your boys?

MOTHER: I miss them every day.

               FOR YEARS I WONDERED
               HOW I HAD FLOUNDERED
               WAS ALL THIS FATE AND FADDER?
               DID ANY OF THIS MATTER?

I STUMBLED WESTWARD
I FOUND THIS WRECK HERE
THE HOUSE OF BOREALIS
A HOME FOR THOSE WHO HAD NONE
LIKE ME

Scene 9

Later that night, LEVI and MOTHER are getting ready for the performance. STAR is looking at all the dresses, wigs, and jewels.

MOTHER: Are you gonna let us make you up tonight? You have the figure and the face, but do you have the nerve?

STAR: I don't know… I'm trying to think of a persona first, you know? Like… who do I wanna be with my balls tucked up inside of me?

MOTHER: *(Laughs.)* You're a freak. But darling, your persona will be revealed to you once you are made up. So don't get ahead of yourself.

STAR: Okay, I'll do it!

MOTHER: Great. Wash your face, then. I don't want my makeup on your oily-ass skin. And glue your brows down with that glue stick in there. Against the grain, hunny! And then comb them flat.

STAR exits to the bathroom down the hall to wash their face and do eyebrows.

MOTHER: He's a peach.

LEVI: I know, right?

MOTHER: You've been spending some time with him.

LEVI: I like him.

MOTHER: Uhhh, don't you think I know that?

            They laugh.

LEVI: But he's nervous and slow to open up.

MOTHER: He has a special light, you know? The kind that won't be put out no matter how hard the world tries.

LEVI: I guess his name is fitting.

MOTHER: STARWALKER... in the House of Borealis? The nerve...

LEVI: The gall...

MOTHER &
LEVI: The gumption.

            STAR comes back in the room, fresh faced, and smiling with a bit of a bounce in his step. LEVI gets up and passes STAR as he leaves the room.

MOTHER: Okay, enough eye-fucks—come and sit down, honey. I'll teach this to you once and then you're on your own. We're going to start with some foundation, you just lather it on, baby, be generous with it. Oh God, don't pound yourself with it. Here, just dab gently.

STAR: Like this?

MOTHER: Good. That's it. How long have you lived out there?

STAR: A couple years.

MOTHER: So you know how to survive on the streets?

STAR:	It's the only thing I'm really good at.
MOTHER:	Ain't nothing wrong with that.
STAR:	But I'm not just turning tricks for money. Broken people helping broken people.
MOTHER:	Uhh, a modern-day Mother Teresa.
STAR:	So kind, so selfless, healing the world one john at a time.
MOTHER:	For the low, low price of 19.99.
STAR:	Do you think people are paying me in pennies? I don't think so.
MOTHER:	Well ,that's good to hear. A lot of my children end up here in rougher shape than how you found us.
STAR:	I've been finding my way on my own for a few years now, so it's nothing new.
MOTHER:	You should know, Levi is my favourite kindhearted child. You break his heart, I break you. Do we understand each other?
STAR:	Yes, Ma'am.
MOTHER:	Good.
STAR:	Hey, Mama. How do you think I'll do?
MOTHER:	In all my years of being a fierce, fabulous, and give-no-fucks Queen I have never met anyone like you. I want you to fucking soar, honey.

STAR smiles. There's a knock at the door.

Yeah?

MICHAEL enters.

MICHAEL: *(To STAR.)* Look at you! About time! *(To MOTHER.)* Cookie is having a breakdown downstairs, she's strung out on something. Can you come and sort her out?

MOTHER: Sort her out your damn self, you don't need me.

MICHAEL: Someone called the cops on her, and they wanna talk to the owner of the house to make sure she lives here.

LEVI enters with STAR's dress.

MOTHER: Oh, Jesus Christ! I'll come. Levi, honey, can you continue in my absence? Make him a pretty girl.

LEVI: Sure.

MOTHER: Thanks, baby.

MICHAEL and MOTHER exit. LEVI tucks himself up close to STAR; there's some nervous laughter, but after a moment STAR calms down, and LEVI continues where MOTHER left off.

LEVI: Okay, now just close your eyes and I'll take over.

STAR: Hmm… take over.

They laugh again.

LEVI: Don't make me laugh, I'll fuck it up.

STAR: Mother would be so mad.

LEVI: Wasting my fucking makeup! For this shit! Okay, okay, okay. This is a black eye pencil to create a new crease. I'll draw it in the socket line, not into the actual eyelid, to create more space. This is your eyeshadow brush. This is your blush brush.

<u>7. GOD IN DRAG, YOU'RE BEAUTIFUL</u>

LEVI: THIS IS AN EXTENSION OF
IT'S THE EXPRESSION OF
WHO YOU WERE ALWAYS MEANT TO BE

THIS IS A DEFIANCE OF
IT'S A REJECTION OF
THE RULES OUR BODIES MADE FOR US

AND NOW BEYOND WHAT THEY EXPECT
IT'S A PERFECT FIT
IT'S THERE, RIGHT THERE, INSIDE OF YOU

AND NOW LET OUT YOUR FEMININE
LET YOUR FABULOUS WIN
YOU'RE GOD IN DRAG, YOU'RE BEAUTIFUL
GOD IN DRAG, YOU'RE BEAUTIFUL
GOD IN DRAG, YOU'RE BEAUTIFUL

YOU'RE BEAUTIFUL
YOU'RE BEAUTIFUL
YOU'RE BEAUTIFUL

Once LEVI is done, he stands and turns STAR to face the mirror.

LEVI: Open your eyes.

STAR opens his eyes.

STAR: No way! I'm a pretty girl!

LEVI: Let's get you in the dress.

STAR: Wait, you remember a while back when I was telling Mama about my name and where I come from?

LEVI: Yeah, some Native thing.

STAR: Oji-Cree.

LEVI: Right, sorry, Oji-Cree…

STAR: Is there a way of fitting that into all of this? Or is it just about the dress, and makeup, and hair?

LEVI: It can be whatever you want it to be.

STAR: Okay, well, I found this back there in Mother's closet. She said she was going to throw it out…

STAR pulls out the large sequined Las Vegas style showgirl's headpiece.

She said it was some old showgirl outfit, but it reminds me of something else. It means something different to me, you know.

LEVI: Sure.

STAR: Do you think it'll work?

LEVI: It'll work, Star.

They grab the dress, heels, and headpiece and start to put it all on.

Scene 10

Backstage, LEVI is putting the final touches on STAR's look in drag, finishing with the headpiece.

STAR: I AM THE DEPICTION OF
BEAUTY IF THERE EVER WAS
I'M WHAT I ALWAYS DREAMED I'D BE

I AM THE CHOSEN FEW
WHO SEE THEMSELVES AS TWO
I FEEL THEM NOW, THEY'RE HERE WITH ME
FEEL THEM NOW, THEY'RE HERE WITH ME

STAR is looking out through a part in the curtain at the performance happening onstage, singing encouraging words to themself, trying to muster up the courage to take the stage.

AND NOW FEMME BOYS REPRESENT
MUST BE CREATOR SENT
I HEAR HER, NOW YOU'RE BEAUTIFUL
HEAR HER NOW, YOU'RE BEAUTIFUL
HEAR HER NOW, YOU'RE BEAUTIFUL

WHY'D THEY SAY IT WAS WRONG?
WAS THERE SOMETHING WRONG WITH ME?
THAT I CAN'T SEE
IS IT WORTH LOSING ALL I EVER KNEW
OF A FAMILY?

QUEENS start coming backstage from the performance in progress onstage, they bustle around STAR and don't give STAR much attention. They're mid-show and have things to do.

I AM THE IMAGE OF
THE PERFECT IMAGE OF
WHO I WAS ALWAYS MEANT TO BE

NOT THE USUAL IMAGE OF
THE BROKEN IMAGE OF
WHAT PEOPLE EXPECT ME TO BE

> *MOTHER sees STAR and is blown away. MOTHER waves to the other QUEENS to come around and circle up to give encouragement.*

MOTHER: AND NOW BEYOND WHAT THEY EXPECT
IT'S A PERFECT FIT
IT'S ALWAYS BEEN INSIDE OF YOU

LEVI: AND NOW LET OUT YOUR FEMININE

STAR: LET YOUR FABULOUS WIN

LEVI: YOU'RE GOD IN DRAG, YOU'RE BEAUTIFUL

STAR, LEVI &
MOTHER: GOD IN DRAG, YOU'RE BEAUTIFUL

ALL: GOD IN DRAG, YOU'RE BEAUTIFUL
YOU'RE BEAUTIFUL
YOU'RE BEAUTIFUL
YOU'RE BEAUTIFUL

> *MOTHER goes out through the curtain and the QUEENS leave STAR alone to make an entrance. LEVI stays behind a minute longer, gives STAR one last look—perfection—and then blows a kiss and leaves. STAR stands behind the centre of the curtains, and, with a flourish, they open.*

Scene 11

> *Onstage at the House of Borealis, MOTHER enters.*

MOTHER: All right, you nasty bitches. We have some of my children who have never done this before, so I want you to remember your first time. It was painful, raw, and… sorry, I'm talking about another kind of first time.

> *Drum kick.*

Okay, shut up, it wasn't that funny. Please welcome to the stage, my new child: STARWALKER BOREALIS.

> *STARWALKER is revealed, wearing a long gown with a sparkling star headpiece.*

8. REBELLION SONG [REPRISE]

STAR: WAY HI YEAH HI WAY HI YO
WAY HI YEAH HI WAY HI YO
WAY HI WAY HI WAY HI YO
WAY HI WAY HI WAY HI YO

WHEN I CLOSE MY EYES, I ONLY THINK OF YOU
I WANT TO HOLD YOU SO CLOSE BUT THAT'S WHAT I CAN'T DO
IF ONLY, IF ONLY, THERE HAD BEEN A DIFFERENT STORY
WHAT IF I KNOW A PLACE WHERE DREAMS COME TRUE
WHERE THE HOME THAT I LOST WAS FOUND IN YOU
IF ONLY, IF ONLY, THERE HAD BEEN A DIFFERENT STORY

A DREAM I USED TO DREAM BUT NEVER
THOUGHT IT COULD BE
A HOME I'D FIND GIVING PEACE OF
MIND
NOT UNLIKE A FAMILY
BUT DREAMS THEY SOMETIMES COME
TRUE
YOU CAN'T SORT IT OUT BUT WE'RE
STARTING BRAND NEW

LEVI enters and joins STAR in the performance.

STAR &
LEVI: WHEN I CLOSE MY EYES, I ONLY THINK
OF YOU
I WANT TO HOLD YOU SO CLOSE BUT
THAT'S WHAT I CAN'T DO
IF ONLY, IF ONLY, THERE HAD BEEN A
DIFFERENT STORY
WHAT IF I KNOW A PLACE WHERE
DREAMS COME TRUE
WHERE THE HOME THAT I LOST WAS
FOUND IN YOU
IF ONLY, IF ONLY, THERE HAD BEEN A
DIFFERENT STORY

All QUEENS enter and entertain the audience; they celebrate STAR's debut.

ALL: BEEN A DIFFERENT, BEEN A DIFFERENT,
BEEN A DIFFERENT STORY
BEEN A DIFFERENT, BEEN A DIFFERENT,
BEEN A DIFFERENT STORY
BEEN A DIFFERENT, BEEN A DIFFERENT,
BEEN A DIFFERENT STORY
BEEN A DIFFERENT, BEEN A DIFFERENT,
BEEN A DIFFERENT STORY

> *Backstage. MOTHER, exhausted, is fanning herself frantically, trying to cool down and wake herself up. SISSY goes to her.*

MOTHER: I KNOW WHAT YOU'RE GONNA SAY, SO SAVE IT

SISSY: YOU CAN'T JUST WISH THIS AWAY, OR FAKE IT
WHY WON'T YOU JUST TAKE A BREAK

MOTHER: AND MISS MY SHOW, MY HOUSE, MY VISION FOR US?

SISSY: ITS HARDER TO NOT LET THEM KNOW, THEY WORRY

MOTHER: YOU'RE NOT MY MOTHER.

SISSY: I KNOW.

MOTHER: SO LEAVE IT

SISSY: I CAN'T KEEP LYING FOR YOU

MOTHER: I DIDN'T ASK YOU TO

SISSY: YOU THINK WHAT YOU HAVE CAN'T HURT YOU?

> *MOTHER coughs.*

MOTHER: I can take care of my goddamn self. Now be a dear, and pass me that towel.

> *SISSY passes MOTHER the towel. MOTHER grabs it aggressively and dabs herself gently with it.*

SISSY: Don't go back out there. You're not well.

MOTHER: Don't you tell me what I am.

MOTHER stops SISSY in her tracks, pauses, again dabs herself gently, and hands the towel back to SISSY.

Look. All better.

MOTHER puts on a smile and leaves SISSY to watch the show from the wings. MOTHER walks onstage as if going into battle.

MOTHER: THERE IS HOPE THERE IN THE REBEL-LION NOW

THERE IS STRENGTH THERE COME FOR THE FIGHT

HOPE IS THE MOST REBELLIOUS THING YOU CAN DO

ALL: LET YOUR INNER REBELLION BREAK THROUGH.

The stage pulses with the drumbeat as STARWALKER begins to powwow dance around the stage, teaching and passing on the dance to each of the QUEENS circling around her. The crowd loves her and each reveal on her outfit makes them scream and point with delight. As she dances, time passes, and versions of her drag evolve to become more polished and political. In moments, STAR becomes a protestor on the front lines, then a mother holding a baby in her arms, and finally she steps forward and kneels, holding up her hand and pressing it down onto red paint. She holds her hand up to her mouth and smears the red across her face with an arm up in protest, the QUEENS around her march with STAR in support.

STAR:

WAY HI YEAH HI WAY HI YO
WAY HI YEAH HI WAY HI YO
WAY HI WAY HI WAY HI YO
WAY HI WAY HI WAY HI YO

LEVI
(*Overlapping.*):

WHEN I CLOSE MY EYES I ONLY THINK
OF YOU
I WANT TO HOLD YOU SO CLOSE BUT
THAT'S WHAT I CAN'T DO
IF ONLY, IF ONLY, THERE HAD BEEN A
DIFFERENT STORY

SISSY:
(*Overlapping.*):

SAID IT WOULD BE FUN
SAY YES AND PLAY DUMB
ONLY THIS ONCE
IT WOULD BE A MATTER OF TIME BEFORE
THEY TOOK ONE

MICHAEL·&
COOKIE
(*Overlapping.*):

YOU'RE BEAUTIFUL
YOU'RE BEAUTIFUL
YOU'RE BEAUTIFUL
YOU'RE BEAUTIFUL

MOTHER
(*Overlapping.*):

I KNOW THE PAST HURTS
IT COMES IN FAST BURSTS
SPINNING INSIDE AN ENDLESS LOOP
NOT KNOWING A WAY TO BREAK
THROUGH UNTIL

During the song, LEVI and STAR drag each other upstairs to LEVI's bedroom in the house and use a chair to lock the door.

They take off each other's drag clothes, clean each other's faces, and start to kiss and passionately make out. They dance with each other and are laughing uproariously, loving every part of what they share with one another.

MOTHER,
COOKIE, SISSY,
MICHAEL,
ENSEMBLE
(Overlapping.):   BEEN A DIFFERENT, BEEN A DIFFERENT,
BEEN A DIFFERENT STORY
BEEN A DIFFERENT, BEEN A DIFFERENT,
BEEN A DIFFERENT STORY
BEEN A DIFFERENT, BEEN A DIFFERENT,
BEEN A DIFFERENT STORY
BEEN A DIFFERENT, BEEN A DIFFERENT,
BEEN A DIFFERENT STORY

LEVI & STAR
(Overlapping.):   YOU'RE BEAUTIFUL
YOU'RE BEAUTIFUL
YOU'RE BEAUTIFUL
YOU'RE BEAUTIFUL

Onstage, the QUEENS and MOTHER continue to dance, making the crowd go wild, until MOTHER can no longer keep up. In the final moment of the song, out of breath and exhausted, MOTHER faints.

End of Act One.

Act Two

Scene 1

9. BOTHERED

MICHAEL: COOKIE, YOU WOULDN'T WANT TO BE HER
SHE'S NOT ALL THERE WHEN YOU SEE HER
SNOW QUEEN, NO AMOUNT SHE WON'T SNIFF
NEVER HAD IT TO BEGIN WITH

CHASING THE DRAGON IN THE MOONLIGHT
TOO MUCH JUST TO HIT THE SAME HIGH
LAST CHANCE TO CRAWL OUT OF HER DARK HOLE
DOESN'T HAVE THE SELF CONTROL

SISSY: DOESN'T HAVE THE SELF CONTROL

MICHAEL: DOESN'T HAVE IT

SISSY: DOESN'T HAVE IT

BOTH: DOESN'T HAVE THE SELF CONTROL

SISSY,
MICHAEL
& COOKIE: TELL ME WHY I SHOULD BE BOTHERED
GIVE IT STRAIGHT AND DON'T BE
AWKWARD
WHAT WAS MISSED WAS BEING
FATHERED
BOTHERED, DON'T BOTHER, YOU'RE
BOTHERED

TELL ME WHY I SHOULD BE BOTHERED
GIVE IT STRAIGHT AND DON'T BE
AWKWARD
WHAT WAS MISSED WAS BEING
FATHERED
BOTHERED, DON'T BOTHER, YOU'RE
BOTHERED

COOKIE: TRUST FUND, MICHAEL COMES FROM
MONEY
THIS LIFE HE CHOOSES WHILE IT'S
SUNNY
BAD DAYS HE RUNS HOME TO HIS
MOMMY
SUFFERED, HE SUFFERS THE SUBURBS

CUTE BOY LOOKS SO WELL ADJUSTED
FAKENESS CAKED ON, IT'S ENCRUSTED
CHERUB NEVER TO BE TRUSTED
SHE CAN'T PULL THIS OFF ALONE

SISSY: SHE CAN'T PULL THIS OFF ALONE

COOKIE: SHE CAN'T PULL THIS

SISSY: SHE CAN'T PULL THIS

BOTH: SHE CAN'T PULL THIS OFF ALONE
SISSY,

MICHAEL
& COOKIE: TELL ME WHY I SHOULD BE BOTHERED
GIVE IT STRAIGHT AND DON'T BE
AWKWARD
WHAT WAS MISSED WAS BEING
FATHERED
BOTHERED, DON'T BOTHER, YOU'RE
BOTHERED

TELL ME WHY I SHOULD BE BOTHERED
GIVE IT STRAIGHT AND DON'T BE
AWKWARD
WHAT WAS MISSED WAS BEING
FATHERED
BOTHERED, DON'T BOTHER, YOU'RE
BOTHERED

In the dressing room. STAR and LEVI are getting ready for the Winter Solstice Ball. LEVI is practising his faces in the mirror.

LEVI: I can't believe we're doing this. I told Siss it was a bad idea, but she doesn't listen to me.

STAR: Hey—give it a rest, hon. We're all going through it. There's nothing we can do.

LEVI: There's plenty. Mother needs help, she needs to go get some professional help.

STAR: Hospitals creep me out. I get why Mother doesn't want to go.

LEVI: Like not voluntarily, but in moments like this, when we don't even know what is happening to her. She just keeps getting worse every day.

STAR: She should stay at home if that's where she wants to be.

LEVI: Yeah, and we just carry on, right? As if nothing is happening? As if no one will notice that something is a bit "off," let's say.

> *LEVI throws his eyeliner down on the dressing table and puts his head in his hands. STAR walks over to comfort him.*

STAR: We got this. Mother's going to be fine, and it will be a great Winter Solstice Ball.

LEVI: This is all wrong. I can't do my face the same old way.

STAR: Then don't do it the same old way.

LEVI: Star, we have one hour before the show.

STAR: You said I was supposed to let my experiences shape what I was going to put out there.

LEVI: And your point is…

STAR: You are obviously feeling a lot of things, put that into your drag.

LEVI: Ugh, I'm fucking up my makeup.

> *LEVI buries his head into STAR's stomach, and STAR gives him a gentle hug.*

> *In the other QUEENS' dressing room.*

ALL: RIGHT THERE

SISSY: THERE'S NOTHING SADDER THAN A DRAG QUEEN

WHO DOESN'T WANT TO DO IT ANYMORE

ALL: RIGHT THERE

SISSY: WHEN YOU'VE SPENT YOUR WORKING YEARS

	IN SOMETHING YOU CAN'T ANSWER FOR
ALL:	RIGHT THERE
SISSY:	IF I COULD PINPOINT WHEN IT STARTED WHEN IT STARTED TO GO WRONG
ALL:	IT WAS RIGHT THERE
SISSY:	IF YOU BLINKED YOU WOULD HAVE MISSED IT AND THE MOMENT WOULD BE GONE
SISSY, MICHAEL & COOKIE:	TELL ME WHY I SHOULD BE BOTHERED GIVE IT STRAIGHT AND DON'T BE AWKWARD WHAT WAS MISSED WAS BEING FATHERED BOTHERED, DON'T BOTHER, YOU'RE BOTHERED

TELL ME WHY I SHOULD BE BOTHERED
GIVE IT STRAIGHT AND DON'T BE
AWKWARD
WHAT WAS MISSED WAS BEING
FATHERED
BOTHERED, DON'T BOTHER, YOU'RE
BOTHERED
DON'T BOTHER, YOU'RE BOTHERED

A QUEEN rushes in the door in a panic.
STAR and LEVI freeze. They all exit.

Scene 2

> *In MOTHER's room. It is dark and there are many QUEENS gathered around her bed, but no one is talking; they're all sitting in silence. LEVI and STAR enter. MOTHER is lying lifeless in the bed. SISSY and MICHAEL pull LEVI aside.*

<u>10. SOMETHING WE DON'T KNOW</u>

MICHAEL: It's really bad.

SISSY: She doesn't want us to call an ambulance or go to the hospital.

LEVI: I know. She has said that to me before. Are we all supposed to just sit here and watch her die?

SISSY: If that's what she wants.

MICHAEL: We don't even know what's happening to her.

LEVI: You can tell she's in a lot of pain.

MICHAEL: What could it be?

SISSY: She hasn't smoked or hooked up in over a decade.

LEVI: That's why she should see a doctor. To get some answers.

MICHAEL: We'll stay here with her. I know she wants her children by her side.

WHO RUNS EVERYTHING AROUND HERE?
WHO MAKES SURE WE'RE ALL FINE?
WHO COULD EVER REPLACE HER
AS IF THERE'S A NEXT ONE IN LINE

> *LEVI sits at the head of the bed next to MOTHER.*

ALL: WE DON'T KNOW?

COOKIE: HOW DID IT GET THIS BAD SO SOON?

ALL: WHO WOULD KNOW WHAT TO DO?

COOKIE: THERE MUST BE SOMETHING WE CAN DO?

ALL: DON'T LET GO
THERE MUST BE SOMETHING WE DON'T KNOW.

SISSY: BEING ROUND HERE THE LONGEST
I'VE BEEN BY MOTHER'S SIDE ALL THIS TIME
BUT SHE'S BEEN SO FOCUSED ON LEVI
AND NOT KEEPING ME AT HER SIDE
COME ON
WE DON'T KNOW

ALL: HOW DID IT GET THIS BAD SO SOON?

SISSY: WHO WOULD KNOW WHAT TO DO?

ALL: THERE MUST BE SOMETHING WE CAN DO?
DON'T LET GO
THERE MUST BE SOMETHING WE DON'T KNOW.

> *MOTHER opens her eyes.*

MOTHER: My boys.

LEVI &
STAR: Hey, Mama.

> *She tries to sit up but is too weak and she flops back down on the bed. They try to help her. She coughs.*

STAR: What do you need?

LEVI: We can get you whatever.

STAR: Want some water? Or something to eat?

MOTHER: No, Jesus Christ. *(Pause.)* I wanted to get a better look at you. Both of you.

> *STAR and LEVI try to smile and sit back down on the bed.*

LEVI: Oh.

MOTHER: You all look fabulous. Nothing like your mothers made you. But just like your mother made you. *(To STAR.)* And did I not say you had the cheekbones to pull off any look?

STAR: You did, Mama.

MOTHER: *(To LEVI.)* And did I not tell you to show her everything you know?

> *She coughs.*

LEVI: You did, Mama.

MOTHER: Ugh, I can't stand it with the long faces. If you are going to sit there and frown, you better snatch that makeup to conceal it.

> *They smile and chuckle only a bit.*

LEVI: You're not looking so good.

MOTHER: Don't you think I know that? But if you're going to get dressed up, you have to perform. Wasting makeup at my expense? Are you trying to stop my heart?

LEVI: We wanted to be with you.

MOTHER: You need to do what you love. That's the best
             way to be with me. I'm in all of what you love.

             IN TIME YOU'LL SEE IT TOOK ALL OF ME
             TO SHAPE THIS HOUSE HERE FOR YOU
             IT WAS THE TIME I SPENT FINDING
             THOSE WHO WERE MEANT
             MEANT TO TURN US INTO SOMETHING
             BRAND NEW

             I WANTED YOU ALL TO SEE YOU THE
             WAY I SEE
             THAT THE WORLD OUTSIDE DON'T GET
             I WANTED EVERYTHING LEFT
             CARRY ON WITH THE REST

             UNDER LEVI'S LEAD
             YOU ARE SURE TO SUCCEED
             YOU'LL TURN IT INSIDE OUT
             TURN IT OUT FOR ME

             *After a while, one by one, the QUEENS get
             up, kiss MOTHER's forehead and leave,
             leaving only LEVI and STAR at her side.*

ALL: WE DON'T KNOW

MOTHER: AND FOR ALL OF YOU

ALL: WHO WOULD KNOW WHAT TO DO

MOTHER: WHO KNOWS WHAT YOU'RE GONNA
             DO

ALL: DON'T LET GO

MOTHER: ALL OF YOU

ALL: THERE MUST BE SOMETHING WE
             DON'T KNOW

LEVI lingers a second longer in the doorway, then exits down the hall.

Scene 3

At the Winter Solstice Ball, on the small stage at the House of Borealis. The look is "snow globe extravaganza" but this performance feels different; there is a charged energy in the room and performances that are on the edge of breaking.

11. WHEN WE FALL (WINTER SOLSTICE BALL)

ALL:

WINTER, WINTER, WINTER
SOLSTICE BALL
SOLSTICE BALL
SOLSTICE BALL
AND LIKE WE'VE ALWAYS WON
WE SHOW YOU HOW IT'S DONE

STANDING TALL
WOH WOH

WE'VE COME A LONG, LONG WAY
NOT BLAMING YESTERDAY
SEE WHAT'S LEFT IN ME

OUR GLAM, OUR LOOKS ARE SWEET
OUR FACES, GODS HAVE BEAT
ALL THAT'S IN BETWEEN

SOLSTICE BALL
AND LIKE WE'VE ALWAYS WON
WE SHOW YOU HOW IT'S DONE
STANDING TALL
WOH WOH

> *SISSY, LEVI, and COOKIE exit the stage. Backstage, SISSY confronts LEVI as COOKIE is pretending to look through the curtain to the stage. She overhears everything.*

SISSY: Don't do it.

LEVI: Siss, this isn't about you. Stay out of it.

SISSY: If it has anything to do with the man upstairs, then it has something to do with me.

LEVI: Don't make it about Mother. We know that's not what this is really about.

SISSY: That's all I'm talking about.

LEVI: Sure it is. I know you got your nose out of joint when Mother asked me to be the new leader of the house.

SISSY: You're not telling me what to do.

LEVI: Guess she wanted someone dependable taking care of things around here.

SISSY: You're a fucking asshole. You know that?

> *COOKIE, in a moment alone backstage, while SISSY and LEVI continue arguing.*

COOKIE: WHEN MOTHER IS GONE WHO WILL BE THERE?
WHO WILL BE THERE TO TAKE CARE?
ONLY SAFE PLACE I HAVE FARED ON MY OWN

I CAN FEEL MYSELF START SPIRALLING
NEEDING SOMETHING TO NUMB THE PAIN

TAKE THESE TRAGIC THOUGHTS AWAY
FROM ME
FROM ME, TAKE THEM FROM ME

FAILURE
JUST LIKE YOU ALWAYS DO
BREAK WHAT YOU PROMISE, TOO
FAIL FAIL FAILURE

> *COOKIE goes onstage for her duet with MICHAEL, who is performing. COOKIE is spinning and twirling MICHAEL around her. Backstage with LEVI and SISSY in mid-conversation. STAR enters.*

STAR: Jesus Christ, the tension back here.

LEVI: It's over now.

SISSY: No, it is not.

> *LEVI takes out his cell phone and starts to dial 911. SISSY reaches over to take it from his hands, and they start struggling over the phone.*

LEVI: Get off me.

SISSY: Give me that.

LEVI: Are you fucking serious?

SISSY: I just need a minute!

STAR: Whoa, stop! Get off him.

> *STAR pulls SISSY off LEVI and separates them.*

SISSY: He's sending her to the hospital when Mother has asked him not to.

LEVI: She is not in her right mind, okay? Are we supposed to take our cues from someone who isn't able to make rational decisions?

STAR steps away from LEVI, immediately triggered.

STAR: You can't make her go to the hospital.

SISSY: Exactly. That's my point. Listen to Star.

LEVI: Listen, I'd love for us all to sit around in harmony and sing "Kumbaya," but that's not going to happen. Someone needs to step in here, and I'm the one who has to do it.

LEVI starts dialling 911. SISSY walks towards LEVI, but LEVI puts his hand out to stop her. STAR is shocked and goes back onstage.

STAR: THEY WILL TRAP ME IF I GO THERE
EVERY HOSPITAL'S THE SAME
I BET THEY EVEN HAVE MY NAME,
SOMEWHERE

ANYWHERE BUT THERE I PROMISE,
IF YOU FORCE ME, I WILL RUN,
IT'S ALL I KNOW,
IT'S ALL I'VE DONE,
I'M DONE, I'M DONE
I NEED TO RUN

RUN
JUST LIKE YOUR FAMILY'S DONE
YOU WERE THEIR CHOSEN ONE
RUN, RUN, RUN

ALL :   WE'VE COME A LONG, LONG WAY
NOT BLAMING YESTERDAY
SEE WHAT'S LEFT IN ME

OUR LOOKS, OUR MAJESTY
Y'ALL CAN'T COMPETE WITH ME
SEE WHAT'S LEFT OF ME
SEE WHAT'S LEFT OF ME
SEE WHAT'S LEFT
WHEN WE FALL.

> *Ambulance lights are seen outside. The performance is over; each QUEEN goes to their own corner. STAR is huddled in the corner and can't even look at the stretcher when it comes in. LEVI escorts the PARAMEDICS to the room upstairs. SISSY, MICHAEL, and COOKIE are huddled in a group on the edge of the stage in various stages of undress. Once PARAMEDICS go upstairs, STAR sneaks out of the house, trying not to be seen. LEVI returns and notices STAR is not there anymore. He looks around for them and then rushes out of the house.*

Scene 4

> *In MOTHER's room, MICHAEL is packing up some of MOTHER's things into a small bag, organizing her dresses, and wigs. She doesn't know what to do with most of it. LEVI enters, he's dressed in all black, the most boy-like we've seen him so far.*

LEVI: Leave it. I'll go through everything and decide what to bring to the hospital.

MICHAEL: I need to be doing something, I think. That's what will help.

LEVI: Michael, darling. It's okay. I've got it. There's some food downstairs, why don't you take a break from this for now? You can always come back to it later.

MICHAEL: Right. I'll do that. Thanks, Levi.

LEVI: We're heading over to the hospital in a bit. Have you seen Star?

<u>12. THIS BROKEN MESS</u>

MICHAEL: No. No one has, sorry.

LEVI: Why would he just leave like that?

MICHAEL: I don't know. Do you want me to bring you up something?

LEVI: No. I'm not hungry. But you—eat something. Please.

> *MICHAEL kisses LEVI's cheek and leaves the room. LEVI takes in the room; this is one of the only times he's been in here without MOTHER. It is quiet, the whole house is unusually quiet.*

LEVI: THIS BROKEN MESS, IT'S ALL FOR YOU
THIS BROKEN MESS TO START BRAND NEW
EVERYWHERE I LOOK I SEE YOUR FACE
EVERYTHING WE HAD WAS IN THIS PLACE

> *All QUEENS appear, grieving, and sing with LEVI.*

LEVI &
QUEENS: WHEN PEOPLE LET YOU DOWN
THEY JUST DON'T CARE
THEY KNOW YOU'LL BE AROUND

EVEN WHEN HE'S NOT THERE

DON'T LET YOUR DOUBT
SHUT OUT YOUR NEED
YOU CAN'T GO OFF
YOU CAN'T BE FREE

LEVI: WHAT WILL BE LEFT OF A LEGACY?
THIS BROKEN MESS OF A FAMILY

> *He walks toward the door, turns off the light, and shuts the door.*

Scene 5

> *At the park, LEVI and STAR are sitting on the same park bench near where they first met.*

13. <u>LOVED YOU SINCE THE DAY I WAS BORN</u>

LEVI: You have to.

STAR: No.

LEVI: You're so irrational.

STAR: I don't trust them, okay? Hospitals freak me out. I'm not going.

LEVI: Star, what if this is the last time you're able to see Mother?

STAR: She can see me when she gets out. It may not even turn into anything bad.

LEVI: It's bad.

STAR: I know.

LEVI: And you're okay abandoning the house and me?

STAR: What do you want, huh? I'm a runaway. It's what I've always done.

LEVI: That's bullshit.

STAR: What do you know about it?

LEVI: I know that we'd be there for you.

STAR: I can't go.

LEVI: DON'T TRY TO TELL ME THIS IS NOT AS YOU LIKE
DON'T TRY TO TELL ME THIS IS OVER
WHEN I TRY TO TELL YOU ALL THE THINGS YOU DO RIGHT
WHEN I TRY TO TELL YOU ALL THIS SOBER

I TELL YOU THAT I LOVED YOU SINCE THE DAY I WAS BORN
I TELL YOU THAT I LOVE YOU WHEN MY HEART KNOWS FOR SURE

STAR gets up and starts to walk away.

WHERE IS THE MAN WHO I MET CRUISING THE PARK?
WHERE IS THE MAN WHO KNEW TO BE THERE?
IF I TOLD HIM NOW DO YOU THINK HE WOULD WALK OUT?
WHAT WOULD HE THINK OF WHAT YOU'RE SAYING?

I TOLD YOU THAT I LOVED YOU SINCE
THE DAY I WAS BORN
I TOLD YOU THAT I LOVED YOU WHEN
MY HEART HAS BEEN TORN

STAR: When I was young, whenever I'd run away, they'd always bring me back to a hospital and lock me in a room for a checkup.

LEVI: Okay, but checkups are a good thing... to make sure you were okay.

STAR: They would lock me up with the other strays, away, out of sight. No food. Water. Or any idea of when we'd get out of there. Sometimes I don't know if I was trapped in that room for 24 hours at a time or 24 years. That's how long it felt in there. I can't go back. I'm not that far out of the system. What if someone recognizes me and takes me back? I'd never see you again or anyone from the House of Borealis.

LEVI: Come with me then.

STAR: It's different for me in places like that.

LEVI: She needs you to come. (*Pause.*) I need you to come.

> *STAR is still full of fear and shakes their head "no."*

LEVI: I CAN'T BELIEVE YOU
I REALLY THOUGHT THAT YOU WOULD STAY,
BET YOU THINK I DIDN'T CARE MUCH ANYWAY.

LEVI: (*Overlapping with STAR's part.*)
                         I CAN'T BELIEVE YOU
                         I REALLY THOUGHT THAT YOU WOULD
                         STAY,
                         BET YOU THINK I DIDN'T CARE MUCH
                         ANYWAY, ANYWAY, ANYWAY.

                         I CAN'T BELIEVE YOU
                         I REALLY THOUGHT THAT YOU WOULD
                         STAY,
                         BET YOU THINK I DIDN'T CARE MUCH
                         ANYWAY, ANYWAY, ANYWAY, ANYWAY.

STAR: (*Overlapping with LEVI's part.*):
                         I NEVER
                         I NEVER ASKED FOR YOU TO CARE
                         THIS MUCH ANYWAY
                         I NEVER I NEVER
                         I NEVER ASKED FOR YOU TO CARE THIS
                         MUCH ANYWAY ANYWAY ANYWAY
                         ANYWAY
                         I NEVER I NEVER I NEVER
                         I NEVER ASKED FOR YOU TO CARE
                         THIS MUCH ANYWAY ANYWAY ANYWAY
                         ANYWAY

BOTH: WOH, WOH, WOH, WOH
                         WOH, WOH, WOH

                         STAR leaves the park.

LEVI: I TOLD YOU THAT I LOVED YOU SINCE
                         THE DAY I WAS BORN
                         I KNOW IT SOUNDS CRAZY WHEN OUR
                         HEARTS HAVE BEEN WORN

                         LEVI sits alone on the park bench and cries.

Scene 6

At the House of Borealis, the next day. They're in rehearsals for the new show that LEVI will be directing, replacing MOTHER. Everyone is wearing rehearsal clothes, lighting is not done, the whole energy is feeling very flat overall. LEVI is directing on the fly and is changing the staging as they go. The QUEENS are not impressed and are visibly frustrated.

14. WHAT THEY DON'T KNOW ABOUT YOU [Reprise]

ALL:
POSE, POSE, POSE
AND HIT THE FLOOR
POSE, POSE, POSE
THEY'RE WANTING MORE
GIVE A POSE, POSE, POSE
REACH FOR THE SKY
THAT POSE, POSE, POSE
WILL GIVE THEM LIFE

THAT POSE

LEVI: All right, you nasty bitches. We have some of my children who have never done this before...

ALL: THAT POSE

LEVI: ...so I want you to remember your first time...

ALL: THAT POSE

LEVI: ...It was painful, raw, and... sorry, I'm talking about another kind of first time.

ALL: THAT POSE

Drum kick.

LEVI: Okay, shut up.

MICHAEL enters the stage and whispers something into LEVI's ear.

(*To the QUEENS.*) Okay, take five.

COOKIE: Thank you, five.

LEVI: (*To MICHAEL.*) When did you hear about this?

MICHAEL: Just now. Some of the Queens are already on their way to the hospital.

LEVI: Right now? Can it wait until after rehearsals?

MICHAEL: The doctors said we should all head over right away.

LEVI: I know… it's just…

MICHAEL: I'm heading to the hospital…

LEVI: I told Star to meet me here.

MICHAEL: Come on. Wake up. Star is not coming.

LEVI: I told him I'd wait.

MICHAEL: Then you'll be waiting forever.

MICHAEL exits. LEVI leaves the house and back out onto the steps where he first said goodbye to STAR.

<u>15. IN THE STARLIGHT [REPRISE]</u>

ALL THIS TIME WITH HIM AND HE'S NO
MORE, I CAN'T FEEL HIM
THESE NIGHTS WITHOUT HIM FEEL LIKE
FOREVER AND A DAY

THESE NIGHTS WITHOUT HIM BUT
PLEASE LET US FIND A WAY

IN THE STARLIGHT, OF MOONLIGHT,
WITHOUT HIS LIGHT? I'LL NEVER BE
THE SAME.
I FELL HARDER INTO HIM
I TANGLED UP IN HIM
TAKE THE WORLD I HAD BEFORE AND
GIVE ME MORE
IN THE STARLIGHT

Scene 7

In the park. STAR is pacing back and forth in clear search of something, frantically searching for the answers through conflicting worlds that are colliding.

16. SOAR

STAR: YOU SAID ALL THE WORDS I NEEDED
MADE UP THE RULES AND SAID I
CHEATED
SAID YOU LOVED ME, SAID YOU LOVED
ME HARDER

BROKE DOWN ALL THE WALLS I SET UP
BROKE MY HEART AND SAID YOU'RE
FED UP
CHOSEN FAMILY, CHOSE ME, RAN FROM
ME
USED ME UP LIKE ALL THE MEN WHO'VE
COME BEFORE
NO, IT'S NOT THE FIRST TIME I'VE
FOUND MY WAY ALONE

SO I GUESS THIS MIGHT BE MY HOME

TAKE BACK LOVE YOU OFFERED WITH
ITS STRINGS
IT'S NOT WORTH ANYTHING WHEN I
KNOW TALK IS CHEAP
YOU SEE ALL THIS PAIN AND YOU HAVE
SYMPATHY
BUT DON'T CONFUSE THAT NEED AS
CALL TO RESCUE ME, PLEASE

RUN AWAY FROM THE HURT UNSPOKEN
RUN AWAY FROM THE CARE THAT'S
BROKEN
SAVE ME, LOVE ME, PUSH AND SHOVE
ME HARDER

SURVIVE THE SYSTEM BY BEING
SCRAPPY
FORGET THE HOME THAT MADE YOU
HAPPY
TURNED AROUND, AROUND, AND NO
ONE'S FOUND
STUMBLING ROUND, AND ROUND, AND
WHO I FOUND
A BOY THAT I NEVER MET ONE LIKE
THIS BEFORE
I SWEAR HE LOOKED AT ME LIKE HE
SAW SOMETHING MORE

ALL MY LOVE I OFFERED NOT KNOWING
HOW
IT'S WHAT'S UNSPOKEN NOW
I SEE WHAT'S BROKEN DOWN
I COULD NEVER BE WHO YOU REALLY
NEEDED ME TO BE
'CAUSE WHAT IS MESSED UP IN ME

I NEVER LET THE WORLD SEE, THE TRUE
ME.

RUN, RUNAWAY
LIKE ALL THOSE WHO RAN FROM YOU
THEY WEREN'T ABLE TO PULL THROUGH

WHAT IF? WHAT IF I'M WRONG?
IF I'VE SEEN MOTHER FOR THE LAST
TIME
I NEED TO GO BE BY HER SIDE
I WASN'T MEANT TO RUN AND HIDE

ALL THAT'S LOST MAY NOT BE SEEN 'TIL
IT'S GONE
THERE'S ONLY HINTS THAT IT'S WRONG
WHEN LOOKING BACK FROM AFAR
WASTING TIME YOU FELT WOULD
NEVER COME TO AN END
IT'S AN UNWELCOME FRIEND THAT
YOU LEARN TO LIVE THROUGH, DON'T
YOU?
I WANNA BE THERE FOR YOU

GAVE ME A HOME I'D NEVER KNOWN,
STAR
SHOWN ME A LOVE I THOUGHT I'D
OUTGROWN
GAVE ME A SPARK I NEVER SAW BEFORE
SHOWED ME THAT I COULD FUCKING
SOAR.

> *He leaves the park and runs towards the hospital.*

Scene 8

In the hospital room. MOTHER is in a bed with QUEENS gathered around. She's awake and they are managing to make her laugh.

MICHAEL: And she walked in with a blue high heel and a blue rhinestone flip-flop. I thought she was going to fall flat on her face after two steps.

They all laugh. LEVI looks at the door, waiting.

SISSY: He'll come.

LEVI: I don't even know why I'm waiting. He won't come.

MOTHER: It is better if he doesn't see me like this. I look like an alien from outer space with these tubes attached to me.

SISSY: An alien would have a better complexion.

They all laugh.

MOTHER: Bitch.

They all stop laughing as the door to the hospital room opens. STAR enters with a bag and a drum slung around his shoulder.

LEVI: Took you long enough.

STAR: Hey.

STAR gives a little wave to LEVI, who waves back.

LEVI: I thought you weren't going to set foot in a hospital.

STAR: I needed to remember who I was, and what I had to offer.

He goes over to the bed and gives MOTHER a kiss, tentatively and gently.

Mama, did you know Two-Spirit people have been known to help Elders pass over?

MOTHER: Who are you calling an Elder?

They all laugh and look at STAR.

STAR: I wouldn't dream of it. Are you not happy to see me?

Then MOTHER speaks quietly.

MOTHER: I'm so happy to see you.

STAR: You are the fierce, fabulous, give-no-fucks Drag Queen Mother who took us all in and gave us a home. The one who made us so happy.

MOTHER: Hard to see all of that, when I look like this.

STAR: I can help with that. We all can help with that.

STAR looks to MICHAEL who pulls out the bag STAR brought. STAR takes off their jacket to reveal a woman's ribbon dress and a shawl. MICHAEL is holding a shell and a feather. She hands STAR medicine, and STAR undoes the bundle and puts some in the shell. STAR lights it with a match and fans it with a feather to get it going. MICHAEL sits on the floor in front of the bed. STAR goes over and gets their drum. STAR hands their drum to LEVI, who sits next to MOTHER on the bed.

Follow me.

> *STAR stands next to the bed and with STAR's direction, LEVI begins to drum.*

17. FANCY DANCE

STAR: WAY YA HEY, WAY YA HEY
WAY YA HEY, WAY YA HEY HEY YO

WAY YA HEY, WAY YA HEY
WAY YA HEY, WAY YA HEY HEY YO

WAY YA HEY, WAY YA HEY
WAY YA HEY, WAY YA HEY HEY YO

> *STAR passes the items to the other QUEENS, who hold them in their hands next to the bed.*

WAY YA HEY, WAY YA HEY
WAY YA HEY, WAY YA HEY HEY YO

STAR: *(Call.)* WAY YA HEY, WAY YA HEY
WAY YA HEY, WAY YA HEY HEY YO

> *The QUEENS, one by one, stand and start to sing with STAR. They walk around the bed to MOTHER and take off the top sheet.*

ALL: *(Response.)* WAY YA HEY, WAY YA HEY
WAY YA HEY, WAY YA HEY HEY YO

STAR: *(Call.)* WAY YA HEY, WAY YA HEY
WAY YA HEY, WAY YA HEY HEY YO

> *MOTHER sits up and they wrap the sheet around her and turn it into a long gown. The QUEENS take the blanket from the bottom and stretch it out so it reaches the floor. It becomes a shimmery, sparkly gown that envelops the hospital bed.*

ALL:		(*Response.*) WAY YA HEY, WAY YA HEY
		WAY YA HEY, WAY YA HEY HEY YO

STAR:		(*Call.*) WAY YA HEY, WAY YA HEY
		WAY YA HEY, WAY YA HEY HEY YO

ALL:		(*Response.*) WAY YA HEY, WAY YA HEY
		WAY YA HEY, WAY YA HEY HEY YO

STAR:		(*Call.*) WAY YA HEY, WAY YA HEY
		WAY YA HEY, WAY YA HEY HEY YO

ALL:		(*Response.*) WAY YA HEY, WAY YA HEY
		WAY YA HEY, WAY YA HEY HEY YO

Drums.

STAR:		(*Call.*) WAY YA HEY, WAY YA HEY
		WAY YA HEY, WAY YA HEY HEY YO

ALL:		(*Response.*) WAY YA HEY, WAY YA HEY
		WAY YA HEY, WAY YA HEY HEY YO

STAR:		(*Call.*) WAY YA HEY, WAY YA HEY
		WAY YA HEY, WAY YA HEY HEY YO

ALL:		(*Response.*) WAY YA HEY, WAY YA HEY
		WAY YA HEY, WAY YA HEY HEY YO

Honour beat. STAR does a slow fancy dance while all the QUEENS sit in their positions on the bed watching her in the centre. MOTHER is moved by STAR's dance.

STAR:		(*Call.*) WAY YA HEY, WAY YA HEY
		WAY YA HEY, WAY YA HEY HEY YO

ALL:		(*Response.*) WAY YA HEY, WAY YA HEY
		WAY YA HEY, WAY YA HEY HEY YO

STAR:		(*Call.*) WAY YA HEY, WAY YA HEY
		WAY YA HEY, WAY YA HEY HEY YO

ALL: *(Response.)* WAY YA HEY, WAY YA HEY
                        WAY YA HEY, WAY YA HEY HEY YO

> *Drum stops. The QUEENS are all sitting around the bed, MOTHER is kneeling at the foot of the bed when sparkles fall slowly from above her. STAR continues to dance in another spotlight just beyond the foot of the bed.*
>
> *They turn the hospital room into a stage. MOTHER is ecstatic. At this moment, they are all free.*

The end.